BOBBY ORR

PHOTO CREDITS
Carl Skalak, Jr.: pp. 15, 21, 27, 29, 31
National Hockey League: pp. 5, 25, and cover
Peter Travers: pp. 7, 9, 11, 13, 17, 19, 23

Published by Creative Educational Society, Inc.,
123 South Broad Street, Mankato, Minnesota 56001
Copyright © 1977 by Creative Educational Society, Inc. International
copyrights reserved in all countries.
No part of this book may be reproduced in any form without written
permission from the publisher. Printed in the United States
Library of Congress Cataloging in Publication Data

Smith, Jay H.
Hockey's legend — Bobby Orr.
SUMMARY: Describes Bobby Orr's legendary ten-year career with
the Boston Bruins.
1. Orr, Bobby, 1948-   —Juvenile literature.
2. Hockey players—Biography—Juvenile literature.
[1. Orr, Bobby, 1948-   2. Hockey players] I. Title.
GV848.5.07S6   796.9'62'0924 [B] [92]   76-45862
ISBN 0-87191-590-1

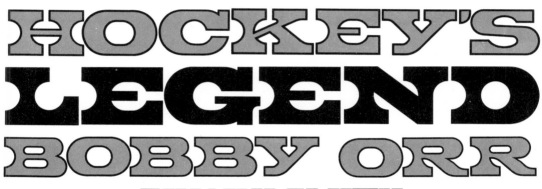

HOCKEY'S LEGEND BOBBY ORR

BY JAY H. SMITH

CREATIVE EDUCATION/CHILDRENS PRESS

4

One day in the summer of 1976, fans of the Boston Bruins heard some very bad news. The news did not surprise them. They had been expecting it for a long time. But that didn't make it any easier to take. For months, they had known that Bobby Orr would be leaving the Bruins after the 1975-76 National Hockey League (NHL) season was over.

All along, they had hoped that somehow a miracle would occur and their hero would remain with the team. But now all of their hopes were gone: Bobby had just signed a contract with the Chicago Black Hawks for the coming 1976-77 season.

6

Bruin fans felt sad and gloomy. They had come to love Bobby dearly. For them, he had been the heart and soul of the team for ten exciting years. They just couldn't imagine the Bruins without Bobby there to lead the way across the ice.

The fans' great love for Bobby began in 1962 — long before he ever put on a Boston uniform. At that time the Bruins were the worst team in hockey; and they seemed to have no hope for the future.

Then the discouraged fans heard about the amazing talents of a 14-year-old boy named Bobby Orr, who played on an amateur junior team sponsored by the Bruins. The fans began to pin all their hopes on the boy. They knew that Bobby wouldn't be eligible to play in the NHL until he was 18. But that didn't matter. They started to look forward to the 1966-67 season, four long years away.

10

The Bruins continued to play ragged hockey. For the next three seasons they always finished last. Hoping to keep the fans' interest alive, Bruin officials often talked about Bobby's progress in the amateur league. The Boston general manager even claimed he wouldn't trade Bobby for the entire Toronto Maple Leaf team.

Soon the fans regarded Bobby as a miracle-worker in whose hands a hockey stick became a magic wand. They were sure that he would save the Bruins' team some day. And they began to call him Super Boy.

Time passed by swiftly. The magic moment came at last — Bobby was ready for the NHL. In his first home game, the young defenseman scored a beautiful goal from the blue line. The wildest dreams of his fans had begun to come true.

When the 1966-67 season was over, Bobby was named Rookie of the Year. He made the Second All-Star team.

Harry Howell of the New York Rangers received the James Norris Trophy as the league's best defenseman that season. When he accepted the trophy, Howell said, "I'm glad I won this award now because I've got a feeling that from now on it's going to belong to Bobby Orr."

14

Despite Bobby's fine individual performance that year, Boston still finished last. But this time, the fans weren't too disappointed. They felt that better days were ahead.

An important trade during the off-season brought Phil Esposito, Ken Hodge and Fred Stanfield to the team. Bobby and his new teammates were fired up. When the 1967-68 season ended, the Bruins had made the Stanley Cup playoffs for the first time in nine years.

During the season Bobby injured his left knee. He had an operation and then returned to the lineup in time for the first round of the playoffs. But the injury slowed him down. His team was defeated by the Montreal Canadiens four games in a row.

Although he had played in only two-thirds of Boston's games that season, Bobby made the First All-Star team. And as Harry Howell had predicted, Bobby won the Norris Trophy. The shy young star was embarrassed. "I don't deserve it," he said. But everyone else thought that he had earned the award.

At the end of the season, a second operation was performed on Bobby's knee. From then on, he always wore extra-thick padding to protect his fragile knees. Even so, he had to undergo knee surgery three more times before his career with the Bruins ended.

18

Bobby kept improving. In 1968-69, his third season, he scored 21 goals and 43 assists. Both marks were new NHL records for defensemen. This time, when he received the Norris Trophy, Bobby felt he deserved it. And he would win it seven more times before his playing days at Boston were over.

The Bruins made the playoffs again, this time going as far as the semi-finals. In his first three seasons Bobby had done everything expected of him — except lead his team to a Stanley Cup triumph.

20

Shortly after training camp opened for the 1969-70 season, Bruin Captain Ted Green was seriously injured. Bobby was chosen by his teammates to replace him. Bobby pushed the Bruins hard all year long but he pushed himself the hardest. He went on to have perhaps the greatest season any NHL player has ever had. He scored 33 goals, breaking his own record for defensemen. His 87 assists were the most ever made in a single NHL season by any player, regardless of position. Bobby's total of 120 points led the league — another first for NHL defensemen.

Most important of all, the Bruins had won the Stanley Cup at last, defeating the St. Louis Blues in the finals.

22

Bobby received the Hart Trophy as Most Valuable Player and just about every other award the league had to offer that season.

At 22, an age when most players are just getting started in pro hockey, Bobby was already the most versatile player in the NHL. Hockey experts generally rated Bobby the best defenseman in history. And a lot of them were convinced that he was the greatest player of all time.

24

After four years in the NHL, Bobby had become a living hockey legend. His style changed the game. Even great players like Gordie Howe studied his technique. Bobby dominated the game in a way that no other player in history had ever done. Brad Park of the Rangers once said, "When Bobby's on the ice, you're playing against an extra man."

Bobby established the standard by which defensive excellence is measured today. It is a perfect combination of offense and defense. Not only does Bobby lead the attack up the ice, he speeds back to *defend the Bruin goal.*

26

Bobby's moves and fakes are famous. When Bobby was a rookie, Ted Green said, "He's got moves that take the rest of us five years to pick up." Every season Bobby seemed to come up with something more spectacular.

Before frequent knee injuries slowed him down a bit, Bobby was the fastest skater around. He was able to change speed at will, shifting from high to low in mid-flight. His numerous lateral shifts and reverse spins made him extremely difficult to catch.

Defenseman Jim Neilson of the Rangers once said, "You think you've got him lined up for a check, and — whoosh — he's gone again."

After Bobby's great 1969-70 season, his legend continued to grow. He kept on scoring at a great rate. He continued to win many awards and honors for his achievements. And in the 1971-72 season he led the Bruins to victory again in the Stanley Cup playoffs.

Bobby often played when injured, but he more than made up for any handicap with determination. One of his opponents, referring to Bobby's bad knee, once said, "He's better on one leg than most players are on two."

Bobby continued to bring a special kind of grace to the often brutal, brawling world of professional hockey.

Bobby Orr faces an uncertain future. Late in November of 1975 he suffered the most serious knee injury of his career. He was sidelined for the rest of the 1975-76 season. Bobby underwent surgery soon after he was hurt.

As the new season approaches, he is still waiting for the knee to mend. Perhaps Bobby will never be able to play for the Chicago Black Hawks. But his fans feel he will play again. He has bounced back so many times before. Only one thing bothers them — Bobby will be playing for Chicago and not Boston.

BILLIE JEAN KING
O. J. SIMPSON
EVEL KNIEVEL
HANK AARON
JOE NAMATH
OLGA KORBUT
FRAN TARKENTON
MUHAMMAD ALI
CHRIS EVERT
FRANCO HARRIS
BOBBY ORR
KAREEM ABDUL JABBAR
JACK NICKLAUS
JOHNNY BENCH
JIMMY CONNORS
A. J. FOYT

THE ALLSTARS